A Duet With Omar

Albert Joseph Edmunds

In the interest of creating a more extensive selection of rare historical book reprints, we have chosen to reproduce this title even though it may possibly have occasional imperfections such as missing and blurred pages, missing text, poor pictures, markings, dark backgrounds and other reproduction issues beyond our control. Because this work is culturally important, we have made it available as a part of our commitment to protecting, preserving and promoting the world's literature. Thank you for your understanding.

A DUET WITH OMAR

By
ALBERT J. EDMUNDS

With a supplement by
James E. Richardson

"*Christ was a missionary to this island of savages in the cosmic sea.*"
(RICHARD HODGSON to the author, April 1, 1898)

PHILADELPHIA:
INNES & SONS, 129-135 NORTH TWELFTH STREET
1913

CARPENTIER

Copyright, 1913, by
ALBERT J. EDMUNDS

The author is under a pledge to the Simplified
Spelling Board of New York to espouse their cause.
See Buddhist and Christian Gospels, Prolegomena 4.

Clarendon type is used to denote oracles and scripture.

DEDICATED TO MY
JOINT-AUTHORS
ELIZABETH AND MARY INNES
AGED VI AND VIII

"*I'm rooting around in the Bible all the time, like you!*"

———

ALSO TO MY SINCERE CRITICS
ESPECIALLY
JAMES E. RICHARDSON,
ARTHUR AND MADELEINE BRADLEY,
JEANNETTE I. WESTCOTT
AND ELIZABETH H. FRISHMUTH

A Duet With Omar

CANTO I.

1

In days of eld Imagination reigned,
On angel wings were heights divine attained,
   But now we rear cathedrals out of fact:
My heaven-wooing verse by Truth is trained.

2

No priest or wizard, murmuring for hire,
Can wrap the spirit in the final fire,
   But **line by line** and **here and there** we glean
The straws that blaze and all the soul inspire.

3

I saw, saith SWEDENBORG, no earthly hand
Write on a temple for the future planned:
   The things of Faith were heretofore believed:
Now it is lawful that we understand.

4

The Seer of Skara died, and one year more
Beheld the tempest of a world-wide war:
   Strange goblins in the Bay of Boston danced,
Like Northern lights upon a cloudy shore.

5

The wine that Dogberry and Shallow drank,
Who scoft at BUNYAN by the Ouse's bank,
   Had turned to fire and lighted earth and sky,
Burning conceits that unto heaven stank.

6

The planet rolled convulst: not Brandywine
Nor Lexington alone was made divine,
   But Dogger Bank, Azores, Conjevaram,
Till rainbow Stripes and Stars began to shine.

7

In wilder tempest, lo! a DARWIN born,
To teach mankind the meaning of the morn;
   MAX MÜLLER followed with the Sacred Books
And saved religion from an age of scorn.

8

We saw the wrecks of a dissolving Rome
And Alexandria besprent with foam,
   Dasht from a wave of Oriental faith:
We traced a live enigma to its home.

9

Known at Benāres, Balkh and Samarkand,
A story went that all could understand:
   How that a hermit, in the noonday heat,
An opening heaven saw, with angel band.

10

White robes were waved, as in celestial dance,
Unearthly music did the charm enhance;
   The seer inquired what joy the angels knew,
Then deeply heard in Himalayan trance:

11

The Buddha who shall be, the pearl unpriced,
Is born with men to be the Hindu Christ,
   In Sākya town and realm of Lumbinī:
Therefore we glory with a joy sufficed.

12

Research revealed the spectral caravan
Of thought : from Balkh to Antioch it ran,
    Where Luke was learning in a Hebrew
        school
The Gospel he re-wrought and gave to man.

13

In the deep waters of the ancient dark
We dived to find thy lost finale, Mark!
    How Christ appeared to Peter all alone,
Gave him the power, and left him true and
        stark.

14

Neanderthal and Java yielded skulls
From ape-humanity's abandoned hulls,
    Dry on the shores of geologic time:
One fact entire theologies annuls.

15

Then ever and anon thru thought's mad whirl
The voice of Ruskin, blither than a girl,
    Soothed us with music, while a deeper tone
Boomed from the thunderbolts Carlyle would
        hurl.

16

Where shall we turn? Religion we have traced
With TYLOR, FRAZER, from the frozen waste
   Of man's primeval dreams. What seer of
      dawn
The nightmares of the night away hath chased?

17

Lo, MYERS comes, to wrestle in the dark
And fire Truth's tinder with a tiny spark,
   Proving that Man, the million-summered
      fruit,
Dies not the death of saurian and shark.

18

The youth of MYERS ends the Middle Age:
When Science thrust him, in a noble rage,
   Out from the heavenly cathedral porch,
Back thru the screened apse-window climbed
      the sage.

19

If unseen powers erst workt upon the world
In ages far into oblivion whirled,
   Said he, they surely work upon it now:
Search for the Truth in humble things im-
      pearled!

CANTO II.

20

My prolog was the door to homely facts,
Not to Augustines and Theophylacts.
  Be humble, reader, now; descend to earth,
Despise not thou my modern Book of Acts.

21

An instrument is ours of traveling sound,
Whereby we talk the hemisphere around:
  When name and voice are equally unknown,
How can the lost identity be found?

22

JAMES HYSLOP, MAN, to Science devotee,
Has proved that trifles are the only key:
  Along the long dark line the lost is found:
"Don't you remember what you said to me?"

23

Why should the Gospel word the learner shock
Because it names the crowing of the cock?
   A trifle, say you. Nay, 'twas tragedy
Unto the stern Apostle of the Rock.

24

When BUDDHA saw the famed PHILANTHROPIST
In apparition mid the morning mist,
   Known was the ghost to ĀNANDO by praise.
Of SĀRIPUTTO, who did once assist

25

With cheer the benefactor's dying day.
O Ānando, said BUDDHA, no display
   Of mystic art identifies for thee
Our wealthy patron, but plain Reason's way.

26

Ah, gifted chorus, once by MYERS led,
Help me proclaim that none of you are dead!
   GURNEY and HODGSON, SIDGWICK, PODMORE,
      JAMES,
Find me the fire that feedeth more than bread!

27

When past the leader and the queen from earth,
A sound of rain declared an end of dearth:
   The sacred springs were welling once again,
New channels hollowed by an earthquake-birth.

28

The gifted chorus had amast the facts—
Dry, weird, grotesque, but scarred with mountain tracts—
   On whose hot lava-sides the leader strong
Turned the new channels into cataracts.

29

Far in the past the century reposed
Wherein our eyelids never had been closed;
   All were on tiptoe for the final book:
We knew the lofty poet had not prosed.

30

He died, and HODGSON o'er the Testament,
Thus left unended, strenuously spent
   His glorious manhood for the Master gone,
While woman toward the work her labor lent.

31

Reader, three threads of labyrinthine rays
Are all I ask of thee to feel, in ways
   Now new to Science, till a cycle dawn
That shall dispel the darkness and the haze.

32

Whene'er I roam the Massachusetts hills,
It is not seeking for the fame that fills
   Their vales with names like BRYANT, WHITTIER,
But KATE M'GUIRE, who there my fancy thrills.

33

JOHN WILKIE, of Chicago, never went
To Massachusetts, but ofttimes he spent
   A genial evening with a man of health,
OSCAR DE WOLF, born there of long descent.

34

Fate whirled the twain to London; English air,
October-chilled, soon laid John Wilkie there;
   De Wolf attended, gave him shelter, too;
One day, asleep upon a parlor chair,

35

Wilkie, awaking, straightway dreamt he had
Upon his knee a paper writing-pad
   Whereon he wrote, and some deep inward
      urge
To read this message to the doctor bade:

36

Dear Doctor: You remember Kate M'Guire
Who lived with you in Chester? To expire
   In Eighteen-seventy-two her fortune was:
That you in London thrive is her desire!

37

Whereat the seer entranced completely woke,
And turning toward the doctor silence broke:
   "Doctor, behold a message here for you!"
"What do you mean?" the doctor sharply spoke.

38

Without the fear of wrath or jeer, I wis—
No subterfuge, explosive words to miss—
   John Wilkie simply to the doctor said:
"I have a message for you. It is this:

39

Dear Doctor: You remember Kate M'Guire
Who lived with you in Chester? To expire
  In Eighteen-seventy-two her fortune was:
That you in London thrive is her desire!

40

Such was the oracle, and all amazed
The Doctor wildly on the patient gazed:
  "How know you Kate M'Guire and Chester
      town?"
"I know not either!" said the patient dazed.

41

The Doctor answered: *I was born and reared
At Chester, Massachusetts. Long endeared
  To me are all those hills and valleys fair,
But your illusion is a trifle weird.*

42

*From Eighteen-sixty-six to Seventy-three
Northampton was my home. Thence would I see,
  Not far away, my Chester friends again,
And Kate M'Guire ofttimes would wait on me.*

43

Obliging girl she was, and found a pride
In serving me, but in dead days hath died:
  Of her these twenty years I have not thought;
I know not when she past out with the tide.

44

The Doctor mused: Do I remember Kate
M'Guire who lived in Massachusetts State
  With me at Chester? Eighteen-seventy-two
Beheld her die. She hopes me kindly fate!

45

Turn we to HENSLEIGH WEDGWOOD. Eighty-nine
The century told when he beheld a sign:
  An arm and sword from castellated notch
Did thru the talking wood with words
      combine:

46

I killed myself long since on Christmas Day.
Would I had died the foremost in the fray!
  A wounded head was mine in Eighteen-ten,
In the Peninsula. I past away

47

Now four-and-forty years. It was the pen
That killed me, not the sword. My head again
   Pains me whene'er I re-descend to earth,
Thus to communicate with mortal men.

48

I captured Banier; I seized his brand,
And in the fortress found beside his hand
   Plans for defense. Yes, Banier. O my head!
John Gurwood. Failing power. You under-
     stand.

49

Now, Wellington to Gurwood had the sword
Of Banier presented, which award
   Is limned in emblem of heraldic arms.
In later days, John Gurwood, who ignored.

50

His wounded head, and redescribed the fight
Of Eighteen-twelve (his ghostly date not
     right!)
   Was overcome by much unwonted toil,
Reft his own life and sank forgotten quite.

51

Hensleigh and two companions all confest
They wotted not of Gurwood and the crest,
  But knew the Iron Duke's dispatches were
By Gurwood given forth. As for the rest,

52

They wist not even that his name was John.
While we surmise that books could lead them
      on,
  Or lurking recollection, how should thought
Thus guide their minds unless the spirits gone

53

Leave a live memory behind, or haunt
Some region of the soul? Ne'er do they daunt
  Or drive to ridicule, except that half
Of man that lags and fears an idle taunt.

54

Reason our personality dissolves,
Or shows that this with vaster orbs revolves
  Around some central fire, to knowledge
      naught:
No doctrine all the hurlyburly solves.

55

Be patient, Man! The star-lore time is slow,
And like her cycles is the silent flow
   Of all our learning down the centuries:
Millions of minds must think before we know.

56

"A jury of the choicest of the wise
Of many generations" must advise
   The judges with a verdict, but to-day
At least we know 'tis not the soul that dies.

CANTO III.

57

Yet while the feet of Science aye must climb
The endless ladder of eternal time,
   To find the Truth through alchemies grotesque
And false astrologies, the high sublime

58

Attends the poet. Science too he owns,
But all her facts are in the tints and tones
  Of his internal being, made secure
Upon Comparison's foundation-stones.

59

Thus Bucke, the friend of Whitman, wrought
    a tower
Of Cosmic Consciousness, a work of power
  Because the **cloud of witnesses** are called
Who from the minster-turret sound the hour.

60

The seer himself, who wrote the book, began
By beatific vision, rare to man,
  Seen early in mid life, the age of most
Who know the Highest and who lead the van.

61

A London evening with the mellow souls
Around whose names the lettered circle rolls;
  A long dark ride alone; and lo! absorbed,
He saw a glory as of altar-coals.

62

All London was in flames, he surely thought,
And from the chariot-window gazed distraught
   To see what this could be, then straightway
      found
It was himself in conflagration caught.

63

His very head was in a cloud of fire
That burned not, but illumined: earth entire
   And human destiny before him lay
Stretcht as a map. Behold, a mighty spire

64

Of faith in God and Goodness rose within
The soul that ne'er had been conceived in sin,
   But by the Holy Ghost. **All shall be saved,**
For all are brethren of supernal kin.

65

Beyond a peradventure, every soul
Revolves at last within divine control;
   All nature glows alive unto the core,
And Love begins and terminates the whole.

66

The vision faded, but the joy remained,
And this was his religion; theories gained
   By church or search were swampt and whelmed away,
Sunk in the universe anew explained.

67

Then ransackt he the wide historic field
And found that kinsfolk of the soul revealed
   Their answering beacon-lights, which made the Truth
No more mysterious, but a scroll unsealed.

68

The saints of God—the Buddha, Christ and Paul,
Plotinus, Pascal of the fire—do all
   Tell what they heard and saw and inly knew.
Behold the Holy City's outer wall.

69

Such is the book, no story wrought for gold,
But twin to Myers, and as manifold,

Tho rugged, like the Rocky Mountain
    heights,
Where two worlds meet, the newer and the old.

70

In ages hence, when long arcades of Truth,
Seen in perspective from the planet's youth,
    Upbuild the vast cathedral of our thought,
Naught shall remain of savage or uncouth.

71

Allied to Science now for evermore,
The Soul is marching in a holy war,
    And from the minarets of light on high
A world-muezzin doth the music pour

72

That wakes the nations from the brunt of strife
To thought and labor, with enrichment rife,
    And warfare only with the beast within.
Hark! 'tis the rising tide—**Eternal Life!**

NOTES

Verse 2. The greatest promotion of spiritual truth has been made by men who have lived for religion, and not by religion. The work of Myers was exactly of this martyr quality. He was a government school inspector, and worked himself to death in his fifties to re-establish religion upon a scientific basis. The hundreds of cases of psychical phenomena collected by him and his colleagues of the Society for Psychical Research were almost entirely from non-professional sources. The professional teacher of religion or ethics on the one hand, and the paid medium on the other, play a subordinate part. Indeed, they are often actively hostile to this branch of science. The two narratives here versified from the Society's Journal are typical ones. Both are reprinted in the immortal work of Myers. Such experiences, occurring amongst people of all conditions, must, sooner or later, make themselves felt as part of the facts of life.

3 and 4. Swedenborg died in 1772; Boston Tea Party, 1773. The passage versified is from *Vera Christiana Religio* (Amsterdam, 1771, paragraph 508).

5. The allusion is to the Bedfordshire "gentry" and "justices" who dined with Sir Matthew Hale in 1661, and made merry over the fact that their moral and intellectual master was a tinker. (See Bunyan's *Grace Abounding*, near the end.) When probed to the bottom, the American Revolution was an uprising against English snobbery—that coarse assertion of superiority by mere officialism and brutal wealth against character and genius.

The Great Ouse, whereon the boro of Bedford is situated; pronounced *Ooze* (International Alphabet, u:z).

6. For neglected aspects of the American Revolution, see *The Struggle for American Independence.* By Sydney G. Fisher (Philadelphia, 1908), and also his remarkable essay: *The Legendary and Myth-Making Process in Histories of the American Revolution,* read before the American Philosophical Society, April 18, 1912. For the battle of Conjevaram in India, between the English and our French and Muhammadan allies, see London *Notes and Queries,* Feb. 2, 1861. (Pronounce *Con'jevaram''*; International Alphabet, kɒndʒevəræm.)

7. *The Sacred Books of the East.* (Oxford, 1879-1910, 50 vols.)

9. See *Buddhist and Christian Gospels,* Vol. I, pp. 77-89, for the date of this poem, and I, 185-186, for a literal translation.

9 and 12. For the significance of Balkh in the history of religion, see *Buddhist and Christian Gospels,* I, 154; also the author's article: *The Progress of Buddhist Research, with something about Pentecost,* in the Chicago *Monist,* October, 1912 (reading *brothers,* instead of the editorial "brethren," in the last sentence). For the part played by Luke in introducing Hindu elements into the Gospel, see *Buddhist Loans to Christianity* in the Chicago *Monist,* January and October, 1912, reprinted at Colombo. For the problem in general: *The Buddhist-Christian Missing Link,* in the Chicago *Open Court,* January, 1912; and *The Wandering Jew: his Probable Buddhist Origin,* in London *Notes and Queries,* January 18, 1913. These

articles are among the most important things that I have written, and it is my wish that they be reprinted at the end of *Buddhist and Christian Gospels,* in case I should not live to issue a fifth edition. Carl Clemen's useful work on *Primitive Christianity and its Non-Jewish Sources* (Giessen, 1909, in German; Edinburgh, 1912, in English) is thirty years out of date in Buddhist criticism.

11. *Lumbinī* is pronounced *Lŏŏmbinee* in English conventional spelling. (International Alphabet, lumbɪni.)

13. The problem of the lost Mark-ending and the present Mark-Appendix is treated by Kirsopp Lake: *Historical Evidence for the Resurrection of Jesus Christ.* (London and New York, 1907.) See also *The Lost Resurrection Document* in the Chicago *Open Court,* March, 1910.

24. The story of Anāthapi*nd*iko's appearance to Buddha after death was (I believe) first translated into a European tongue in *Buddhist and Christian Gospels.* (Tōkyō, 1905, pp. 204-206; Philadelphia, 1909, II, 195-197; Milan, 1913, p. 266.)

Ānando, Buddha's beloved disciple, pronounced *Ahnundo* (International Alphabet, anəndo).

27. Myers and Victoria both died in January, 1901.

28. The Society for Psychical Research, founded by a band of scholars at the University of Cambridge in 1882.

29. *Human Personality and Its Survival of Bodily Death.* By Frederic W. H. Myers. (London, New York and Bombay, 1903.) The reference to woman is to

the editorial work of Alice Johnson and to the assistance rendered Hodgson by his secretary from 1890 to 1905. *Human Personality,* I, note to preface; II, 616.) The tiptoe expectation was such that the whole edition was sold in three weeks, and London had to call for copies on New York.

32. The case of Katy M'Guire is in the same work. (II, 214-217.)

33. There is a De Wolf Genealogy (New York, 1902) containing accounts of Dr. Oscar and his father. Curiously enough, two stanzas of *Omar* are quoted.

34. "Bronchitis-laden" was my literalistic version, but to this James E. Richardson objected. October, 1895, was the date of Wilkie's illness, and the story was written for the Society for Psychical Research by both witnesses in April and May, 1898.

36. The exact words were: **Dear Doctor—Do you remember Katy M'Guire, who used to live with you in Chester? She died in 1872. She hopes you are having a good time in London.**

45. The case of Hensleigh Wedgwood, brother-in-law to Darwin, and himself a scholar of note, is in Myers II, 161-167. It ought to be rescued from the small print wherein it is read at disadvantage. It is curious that in 1889, the year of Wedgwood's experience, the biographical sketch of Colonel Gurwood in the *Dictionary of National Biography* was passing thru the press. (Vol. XXIII, London, 1890.) The article confirms the planchette.

47. The planchette's words are: **Pen did for me.** Repeated with variations. A sense of humor and a sense of the sublime are equally necessary in these studies.

48. The storming of Cuidad Rodrigo, January, 1812.

50, 51. The Duke of Wellington's Dispatches were edited by Gurwood in 13 vols. (1834-1839.) The work was too much for him after the wound. He was working on the second edition (1844-1847, 8 vols.) when he died.

54. Justice must be done to the problem of our personality's final destiny, upon which the Hindus have done more thinking than all other nations combined.

56. Shelley's Essays.

59. *Cosmic Consciousness.* By R. M. Bucke. (Philadelphia, 1901.) This book was in the press simultaneously with that of Myers, and it is unfortunate that they were then unknown to each other, though Bucke alludes to the previous articles of Myers. Bucke's vision has been popularized by William James in his *Varieties of Religious Experience.*

61. London, England, not to be confounded with London, Ontario, in the life of Bucke.

68. Catholics will remember that the Buddha (known in the calendar as Josaphat) is a saint of the Roman Church (November 27) and of the Greek Church (August 26).
Blaise Pascal, in 1654, had a vision similar to Doctor Bucke's. There is no doubt that it is this

very experience that is meant in the Buddhist texts by the phrase: **entering into the flame-meditation.** For a mythical story about this, see the ascension of Dabbo, the Mallian, first translated in the Chicago *Open Court* for February, 1900, reprinted in *Buddhist and Christian Gospels* (Tōkyō, 1905, p. 192; Philadelphia, 1909, II, 174-175; Milan, 1913, p. 253).

69. Of course Bucke cannot be compared with Myers for scholarship, style or extent, but their aim is one: to re-establish religion upon a scientific basis.

SUPPLEMENT

Wherein the reader is introduced behind the scenes in verse-making

NOTE.—Lacking confidence in his own poetic ability, the author showed the manuscript to James E. Richardson, the poet, to whom are due the following words: *rolled*, in stanza 5; *thru thought's*, in 15; *screened apse*, instead of *vestry*, in 18. Verse 38 was also composed at his suggestion for dramatic effect, as well as 44. *The doctor mused* is Richardson's, tho the rest of the verse is simply my original draft of stanzas 36 and 39, slightly altered.

Mr. Richardson rewrote Canto I from an earlier draft, and his version is appended for the interest of students.

The poets who have influenced me most have been: Longfellow and Campbell (since 1868); Cowper (1869); Gray, Poe, Macaulay and a modicum of Byron (about 1870); Milton and Aytoun (1871); Scott (1873, lyrics earlier); Shakspeare (1874); Calverley (1877); Myers (1878); Tennyson and Wordsworth (1880, but some lyrics earlier); Whittier (1881); Shelley (1884); Matthew Arnold (1898); Burton (1901); Fitzgerald (1912). The *Omar* was read to me by Frank W. Peirson in 1898, but made little impression.

Richardson has been influenced by Swinburne and Rossetti, who have never appealed to me (except one chorus of the former's).

My dear Edmunds:

I have your drafts and have given them a day's full analysis, reaching, unfortunately, the inevitable conclusion: that your own metrical method and mine are so hopelessly dissimilar that I cannot really help you. Whatever criticism I can offer must be from a standpoint so different from yours, that I fear to accept any of it can only do more harm than good. Your own directness and my slow method,—that of crushing dissyllables, feeding in surd adjectives, and generally holding the lines back to the weariest possible elegiac drone,—have little in common. The tempo of your lines and mine, in the one case so sharp and clear and in the other so disguised and thickened with artificial pauses, must, if each of us takes a hand, give the whole thing away. Retaining the end-rhymes, I have recast the whole poem as I should originally have metrified it; using, perhaps, more of the "run-on" structure than is really characteristic of the good rubaiy. So you can see how different our notions of metre really are. I can't overcome the temptation to look at words in the artistic, as against the intellectual sense, i.e., the sound of them as against the meaning; which is very bad all round. If, however, you can use one of my own little tesserals here and there to any effect, by all means do. * * *

               Sincerely yours,
               JAMES E. RICHARDSON.

A DUET WITH OMAR.

In our old days Imagination reigned:
By angel wings were Heaven's vast portals
 gained;
 But now? We raise cathedrals out of fact:(a)
My Heaven-aspiring verse by Truth is trained.

No priest nor wizard, muttering low for hire,
Can whelm the spirit in Hell's ultimate fire; *
 But line by line, lo! here and there we glean
The straws that blaze and our freed souls in-
 spire.

I saw, saith Swedenborg, no earthly hand
Scribe on Life's temple, for high futures
 planned:
 The things of faith were heretofore believed:
Now is it lawful that we understand.

But he of Stockholm passed, and one year more
Saw the storms rise of Change in world-wide
 war:
 Strange figures in the Bay of Boston danced
Like Northern lights upon a cloudy shore.

The planet reeled convulsed; not Brandywine
Nor Lexington alone was made divine,
  But Dogger Bank, Azores, Conjevaram,
Till rainbowed Stars and Stripes rolled forth benign.

In wilder tempests, though, was Darwin born
To show Man's soul the meanings of the morn.
  Max Müller followed, with long-hidden scrolls
To save Religion from an age of scorn.

We saw the wrecks of fast-dissolving Rome
And Alexandria grayed round with foam
  Dashed from green waves of Oriental faith;
We clewed one live enigma to its home.

Known through Benares, Balkh and Samarkand,
The word went round that all might understand:
  How one sad hermit, through the noonday's glare,
Saw Heaven yawn wide with its angelic band;

The white forms as in grave celestial dance
Move in strange ecstasy; pass round, *b* advance

To their unearthly lutings, meanwhile he
Heard icily in his revealing trance:

THE BUDDHA WHO SHALL BE, THE PEARL UNPRICED,
IS BORN WITH MEN TO BE THE HINDU CHRIST,
   IN SAKYA TOWN AND REALM OF LUMBINI:
THEREFORE WE GLORY WITH A JOY SUFFICED.

Our own eyes saw the spectral caravan
Of thought: from Balkh to Antioch it ran,
   Where Luke learned,—pondering in a
      Hebrew school,—
The Gospel soon re-wrought and given to Man.

In the deep waters of the ancient dark
We dived to find thy lost finale, Mark!
   How Christ appeared to Peter all alone,
Gave him the power and left him true and
   stark.

Neanderthal and Java brought us,—skulls
From ape-humanity's abandoned hulls
   Dry on the waste sands of Eternity . . .
One fact . . . entire theologies . . . . annuls.

Sometime, anon through thought's confused,
   blind whirl,

The voice of Ruskin, blither than a girl,
  Soothed us with music, oe'r the undertone
Boomed from the thunderbolts Carlyle would
    hurl.

* * * * * * * * * * * *

Where shall we turn? Religion we have traced
With Tylor, Frazer, from that frozen waste
  Of Man's primeval dreams.   What seer of
    dawn
The nightmares of the night away hath chased?

Lo, MYERS stands forth to wrestle with the
    dark,
And fire Truth's tinder with one imminent
    spark,
  Proving that Man, the million-summered
    fruit,
Dies not the death of saurian and shark.

The youth of Myers ends the Middle age;
When Science thrust him, in ignoble rage,
  Forth from the heavenly cathedral-porch,
Back through the screened apse-window
    climbed the sage.

*Mr. Richardson mistakes my meaning here.

Var:

a But now we raise cathedrals out of fact,

b "pass round"; substitute phrase of equal quantitative value. This used only for phonetic sufficiency.

INDEX OF PERSONS
BY VERSES

Ānando (*flor.* B.C. 500), 24, 25.
Anāthapi*nd*iko (*flor.* B.C. 500), 24.
Augustine (354-430), 20.
Banier (*flor.* 1812), 48, 49.
Bryant, William Cullen (1794-1878), 32.
Bucke, Richard Maurice (1837-1902), 59-68.
Buddha (*circa* B.C. 560-480) 24, 68.
Bunyan, John (1628-1688), 5.
Carlyle, Thomas (1795-1881), 15.
Darwin, Charles (1809-1882), 7.
De Wolf, Oscar C. (1835-19—?), 33-44.
Frazer, James G., 16.
Gurney, Edmund (1847-1888), 26.
Gurwood, John (1790-1845), 45-52.
Hodgson, Richard (1855-1905), 26, 30.
Hyslop, James, 22.
James, William (1842-1910), 26.
Jesus Christ, 13, 68.
Luke (*Saec.* I.), 12.
M'Guire, Kate (died 1872), 32-44.
Mark (*Saec.* I.), 13.
Max Müller, F. (1823-1900), 7.
Myers, Frederic W. H. (1843-1901), 17, 18, 26, 27.

Pascal, Blaise (1623-1662), 68.
Paul (*Saec.* I.), 68.
Peter (*Saec.* I.), 13, 23.
Plotinus (*Saec.* III.), 68.
Ruskin, John (1819-1900), 15.
Sâriputto (*flor.* B.C. 500), 24.
Sidgwick, Henry (1838-1900), 26.
Swedenborg, Emanuel (1688-1772), 3, 4.
Theophylact (*Saec.* XI.), 20.
Tylor, Edward B., 16.
Victoria, Queen (1819-1901), 27.
Wedgwood, Hensleigh (1803-1891), 45-52.
Wellington, Arthur, Duke of (1769-1852), 49, 51.
Whitman, Walt (1819-1892), 59.
Whittier, John Greenleaf (1807-1892), 32.
Wilkie, John E., 33-44.

COMPANION BOOKS

1 **HUMAN PERSONALITY AND ITS SUR-
   VIVAL OF BODILY DEATH.** By FREDERIC
   W. H. MYERS. London, New York and Bombay:
   Longmans, 1903, 2 vols, 8vo.
   Contains the narratives in Canto II

2 **COSMIC CONSCIOUSNESS: a Study in the
   Evolution of the Human Mind.** Edited by
   RICHARD MAURICE BUCKE, [M. D.] Philadelphia:
   Innes & Sons, 1901, 4to. (With portrait, 1905.)
   Contains the narrative in Canto III

3 **BUDDHIST AND CHRISTIAN GOSPELS,
   Now First Compared from the Originals.** By
   ALBERT J. EDMUNDS, M. A. Edited, with English
   notes on Chinese versions, by M. Anesaki, Professor of
   Religious Science in the Imperial University of Tōkyō.
   Fourth edition; being the Tōkyō edition revised and
   enlarged. Philadelphia: Innes & Sons; London: Luzac
   & Co., 1908-1909. 2 vols, 8vo. (Postscript, 1912.)
   Contains sacred texts (which are here versified) literally translated

The same in Italian (No. 21 in Sandron's International Scientific Series: Milan, Palermo and Naples, 1913.)

Printed by Innes & Sons, Philadelphia, for Arthur H. Thomas, Morris
E. Leeds, Arthur N. Leeds, J. Stogdell Stokes and the author

Printed by Libri Plureos GmbH in Hamburg, Germany